Withdrawn

Sports and Activities

Let's Do Karate!

by Carol K. Lindeen

Consulting Editor: Gail Saunders-Smith, PhD

Consultant: Kymm Ballard, MA
Physical Education, Athletics, and Sports Medicine Consultant
North Carolina Department of Public Instruction

Capstone press®

Mankato, Minnesota

Pebble Plus is published by Capstone Press,
151 Good Counsel Drive, P.O. Box 669, Mankato, Minnesota 56002.
www.capstonepress.com

1 2 3 4 5 6 11 10 09 08 07 06

Library of Congress Cataloging-in-Publication Data
Lindeen, Carol K., 1976–
Let's do karate! / by Carol K. Lindeen.
    p. cm.—(Pebble plus. Sports and activities)
    Summary: "Simple text and photographs present the skills, equipment, and safety concerns
of karate"—Provided by publisher.
    Includes bibliographical references and index.
    ISBN-13: 978-0-7368-6358-2 (hardcover)
    ISBN-10: 0-7368-6358-3 (hardcover)
    1. Karate for children—Juvenile literature. I. Title. II. Series.
GV1114.32.L56 2007
796.815'3083—dc22   2006000501

Editorial Credits
Amber Bannerman, editor; Juliette Peters, set designer; Bobbi J. Wyss, book designer; Kelly Garvin, photo
    researcher/photo editor

Photo Credits
Capstone Press/Karon Dubke, cover, 1, 6–7, 9, 11, 13, 14–15, 19
Corbis/Tom Stewart, 4-5
PhotoEdit Inc./Tony Freeman, 16–17, 21

**Capstone Press thanks Master Colby Winkler and Sir Robert Boelter of Mankato, Minnesota, for their
    assistance with this book.**

Note to Parents and Teachers

The Sports and Activities set supports national physical education standards related
to recognizing movement forms and exhibiting a physically active lifestyle. This book
describes and illustrates karate. The images support early readers in understanding the
text. The repetition of words and phrases helps early readers learn new words. This book
also introduces early readers to subject-specific vocabulary words, which are defined in
the Glossary section. Early readers may need assistance to read some words and to use
the Table of Contents, Glossary, Read More, Internet Sites, and Index sections of the book.

Table of Contents

Karate

Kick, strike, and block!

Karate is a martial art

that started in Japan.

Karate is a sport

that is good exercise.

It is also a form

of self-defense.

Karate teaches self-discipline.

Students learn

how to concentrate.

Karate teachers
show students
the right way to
kick, strike, and block.

Karate Gear

Loose pants let your legs
bend and move.
A matching jacket
wraps around your body.

A colored belt shows
how well you know karate.
White is for beginners.
Black is for experts.

Karate Safety

People warm up and stretch
before doing karate.
They don't want to hurt
their muscles.

Pads and shields
help make practice safe.
People remove their jewelry.
A ring or watch
could scratch.

Having Fun

Punch, kick, and block.

Let's do karate!

21

Glossary

block—to stop an action from taking place; in karate, to stop a punch or kick.

concentrate—to think clearly and to put your full attention on something

expert—a person with great skill or a lot of knowledge in something

martial art—a way of fighting and defending yourself; martial arts are practiced as sports.

self-defense—the act of protecting yourself against attacks

self-discipline—control over the way you think and act

shield—an object that gives protection from harm

strike—to hit

warm up—to stretch and exercise gently before harder exercise

Read More

Buckley, Thomas J. *Karate.* Kids' Guides to Martial Arts. Chanhassen, Minn.: Child's World, 2004.

Morris, Neil. *Karate.* Get Going! Martial Arts. Chicago: Heinemann, 2001.

Nevius, Carol. *Karate Hour.* New York: Marshall Cavendish, 2004.

Internet Sites

FactHound offers a safe, fun way to find Internet sites related to this book. All of the sites on FactHound have been researched by our staff.

Here's how:

1. Visit *www.facthound.com*

2. Choose your grade level.

3. Type in this book ID **0736863583** for age-appropriate sites. You may also browse subjects by clicking on letters, or by clicking on pictures and words.

4. Click on the **Fetch It** button.

FactHound will fetch the best sites for you!

Index

Word Count: 119
Grade: 1
Early-Intervention Level: 15